Mysteries

Y0-CAB-540

A

Book

of

Tails

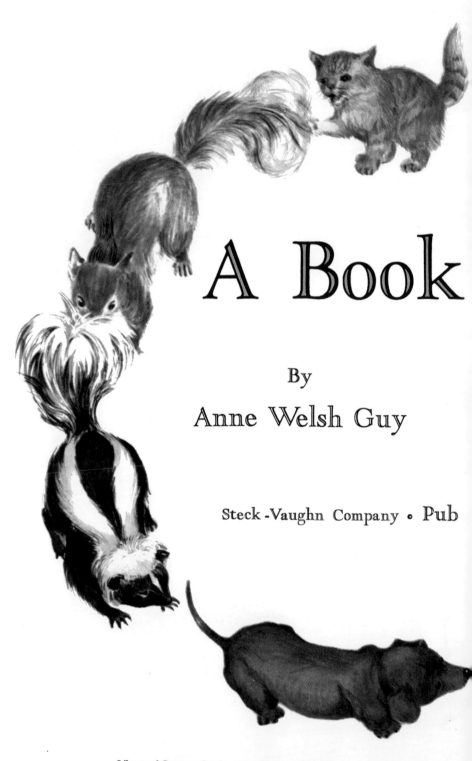

A Book

By

Anne Welsh Guy

Steck-Vaughn Company • Pub

Library of Congress Catalog Card Number 57-6485   Copyright © 1957 by

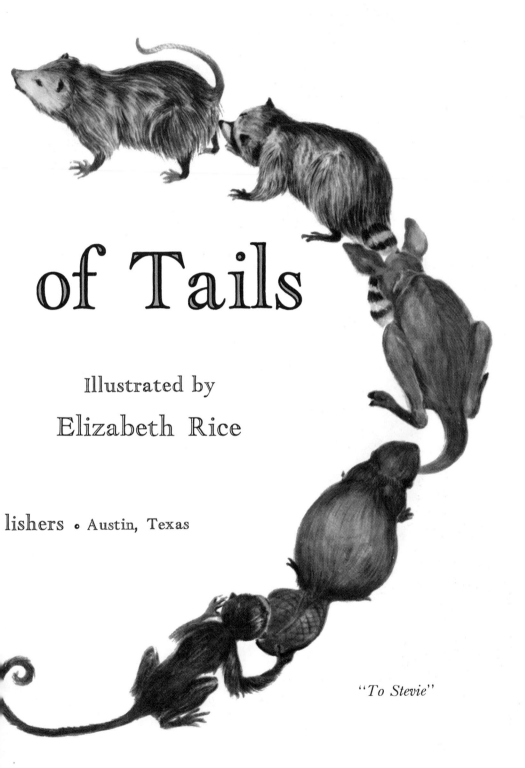

# of Tails

Illustrated by

Elizabeth Rice

lishers • Austin, Texas

"To Stevie"

teck-Vaughn Company Printed and bound in the United States of America

Mother Cat
waves her tail
to and fro, to and fro.
Baby Kitten watches.
She jumps! Pounce!
She gets Mother Cat's tail.

4

"Good baby," purrs Mother Cat.
"Now you know how to catch a mouse!"

Mother Opossum says,
"See me! See me!
See me swing
by my tail?"

"Let us go for a walk, babies.
Get on my back.
 Put your tails around my tail.
  Here we go!
   What fun this is!"

Look at Mother Deer!
It is dark night.
But see the white on her tail?
It shines like a light
in the dark night.
Wig-wag! Wig-wag!
The tail is up!

"Run, babies!
Follow my tail!
After me!
Danger!"

Mother Beaver is making
a house.
See her tail?
It is wide and flat.
She sets herself up
on her tail
while she
makes mud
for her
house.
But—
listen!

Mother Beaver hears something!
Thwack!
Down comes her tail
on the water—
crack!
like the shot
of a gun!
All beavers, run!
Hurry to the water!
Swim under the water
and hide!

11

Jump,
    jump,
        jump!

Here comes
Mother Kangaroo.
What big jumps she takes!

12

Her tail helps her jump.
Then she and her baby
sit down to rest.
Her tail is
a chair.

Old Man Alligator comes
creeping, creeping.
His little eyes are looking, looking.

Do not come too near, little monkey.
Don't tease Old Man Alligator.
Swing! will go Mr. Alligator's tail.
Mr. Alligator's tail is very strong.
It will knock you down.
Then good-by, little monkey.

Frisky little Squirrel sits
in the snow.
But he will not get cold
in the snow.
He combs and fluffs
his bushy tail.

He wraps his tail
around his face
when he sleeps at night.
Then his nose
will not get cold.

His tail is a balancer,
too.
It keeps him from falling
as he sits up
cracking nuts.
How proud the squirrel is
of his bushy tail!

This tiny squirrel is
a flying squirrel.
There he goes.
His tail is like
a parachute.

The tiny squirrel
will not get hurt.
He will not fall, thump!
He will drift to the ground.

What is that puppy doing?
He sees something funny,
    a funny black ball.
        Is it something to play with?
        Something waves. See him?

"Ouch!
     Yipe!
          Yipe!
               Yipe!"
See the puppy run!
His nose hurts.
Porcupine hit the puppy with a swish
     of his tail.
Puppy's nose has fifty or more sharp
     quills in it.

19

This animal is a pocket gopher.
She has very small eyes.
She does not use her eyes much.
She lives underground in the dark.

See her run backwards?
She taps the tip of her tail to the ground.
Tap, tap, tap!
Her tail is a cane, a cane to feel her way
     underground in the dark.
Tap, tap, tap!
Her tail helps her find the way.

Is that a kitten?
It looks like a pretty
kitten,
a pretty black and
white kitten.

Up goes its bushy tail!
Oh, my, oh, my!
Stop! Let it alone!
It is not a kitten.
It is a wood pussy—
    a skunk.
Run away from here.
Run as fast as you can.

Here comes a sly old fox.
What is he chasing?

Poor little
Kangaroo Rat.
Look at the fox's
big bushy tail.

Look at Kangaroo Rat's long thin tail.
The fox's tail stretches out as he runs.
But Kangaroo Rat's tail is longer.
Kangaroo Rat's tail helps him leap away
    from the sly old fox.
Kangaroo Rat can jump 25 feet at one leap.
    The sly old fox will not catch
    Kangaroo Rat.

Look at the cute little raccoon.
He looks like a little bear.
But his tail is too long and bushy
     for a bear.
What is he washing in the stream?
After he washes the frog, he eats it.

Then—
    up the tree
    he runs.
Up, up, up to a nest
    high in the tree top.
He wraps his bushy tail around himself
    like a muff, a black-striped muff.
In his muff the little raccoon sleeps all day,
    snug and warm.

Oh, look! A rattlesnake!
He is going to strike!

Rattle! Rattle! Rattle!
He rattles his tail.
Run, baby rabbit.
Run for your life.

"Mew.
Mew.
Mew."
Is a kitten up
in the tree?
No, it is only a bird,
a bird with a black
cap on its head.
"Mew, mew, mew."
It swings its tail like a kitten,
to and fro, to and fro.
It is the cat bird.
It keeps time with its tail.

Tap, tippy-tap!
Tap, tippy-tap!
Tap, tippy-tap, tap, tap!
That is the red-headed
  woodpecker.
He is hunting for grubs.
See his stiff tail feathers.
The feathers are tipped
  with spikes.
The woodpecker pushes the spikes
  against the bark of the tree.
He digs his sharp claws in, too.
Now he cannot slip.
He can work with his strong beak.
Tap, tippy-tap, tap, tap!

What a big bird!
What long feathers he has!
The bird is a peacock.
Here comes the lady peacock.
When he sees her,
he spreads
his long tail.
It looks like a fan.
A beautiful, beautiful fan.
See him strut!
He shows the lady peacock
his beautiful tail!
He is very proud of it.

33

What is that?
It ran across the path.
It ran so fast.
Oh, there it is.
It is a little lizard.
He is on a rock in the sun.
Let's catch him.
Oh, he is gone!

Up the tree he skitters.
Oh, look!
He has left his tail behind.
The little lizard
    doesn't care.
Soon he will grow
    another tail.

Mother Monkey
  is worried.
Look at her baby.
He is at the very top
  of a tall tree.
He swings and swings
  from the limb of the tree.
He swings by his tail.

"Come down, Baby Monkey.
Please, come down.
You are such a little monkey.
You are swinging so high."

Little Dog
   is not happy.
His tail droops
   down.
He is sick.

When Little Dog is happy, how fast he
   wags his tail!
He holds it up high when he feels well.

When Little Dog is afraid, he puts his tail
between his legs and away he runs,
as fast as he can.

It is a very hot day.
Black Horse stands by the tree.
White Horse stands
    by the tree, too.

They stand side by side.
Black Horse faces one way.
White Horse faces the other way.

Swish,
swish,
swish,
go their tails.
Go away, flies.
Black Horse keeps the flies off White Horse.
White Horse keeps the flies off Black Horse.

41

What little,
  little tails
    the sheep have!
That is because
  the farmer cut off
    the sheep's tails.
He cut the sheep's tails off
  when the sheep were very little.
Tails get full of burrs and dirt.

Burrs and dirt spoil the wool.
The farmer wants the wool to make warm
   clothes.
So off go the tails of the baby lambs!
It does not hurt them, not very much.

Wiggle, wiggle.
Little Tadpole
 wiggles his tail.
That is how he swims.

Little Tadpole has two eyes, and a mouth,
 and a round stomach.
But most of him is tail.

Soon Little Tadpole gets legs
 and funny little arms.

Next, how strange!
What happens then
to
his long tail?

Does it drop off?
No, it gets shorter
and shorter
and shorter,
and then
one day it disappears.
Little Tadpole has become a frog.

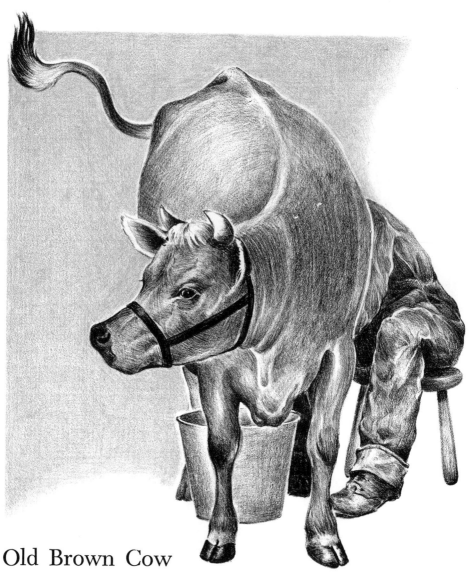

Old Brown Cow
   is hot.
She swishes
   her long tail.
She wants to keep the flies away.
Farmer Bright is milking Brown Cow.
His pail is full of milk.

Ouch!
A big, big green fly
bites Brown Cow.
Swish, her tail swings up.
It hits the green fly.
But it hits Farmer Bright's pail, too.
Down goes the white milk all over the
ground!